604

REEFS

BY SALLY M. WALKER

LERNER PUBLICATIONS COMPANY · MINNEAPOLIS

Lerner Publications Company
A division of Lerner Publishing Group, Inc.
241 First Avenue North
Minneapolis, MN 55401 U.S.A.

Website address: www.lernerbooks.com

Library of Congress Cataloging-in-Publication Data

Walker, Sally M.
    Reefs / by Sally M. Walker.
        p.   cm. — (Early bird Earth science)
    Includes index.
    ISBN: 978-0-8225-6738-7 (lib. bdg. : alk. paper)
    1. Coral reefs and islands—Juvenile literature. I. Title.
GB512.W35 2008
578.77′89—dc22   2006101487

Manufactured in the United States of America
1 2 3 4 5 6 – JR – 13 12 11 10 09 08

CONTENTS

BE A WORD DETECTIVE

Can you find these words as you read about reefs? Be a
detective and try to figure out what they mean. You can
turn to the glossary on page 46 for help.

algae	**carbon dioxide**	**fossils**
atoll	**colony**	**fringing reef**
barrier reef	**coral polyps**	**tentacles**
calcium carbonate	**extinct**	

Many plants and animals live on ridges near the ocean surface. What are these ridges made of?

CHAPTER 1
WHAT IS A REEF?

The ocean floor is full of bumps and ridges. Ridges are narrow, raised parts. The tops of some ocean ridges are close to the water's surface. These ridges are called reefs.

Earth's oceans have several kinds of reefs. Some reefs are made of rock. Others are made of sand. Some are made from the shells of sea animals. Tiny animals called coral polyps (KOR-uhl PAH-lihps) can make a reef too. The polyps have a hard outer frame called a skeleton. Their skeletons join to one another. Together, the skeletons form a coral reef.

Corals are often brightly colored.

Reefs are busy places. Eels and smaller fish live in the spaces inside a reef. So do crabs, starfish, and octopuses. Giant clams grow on top of reefs. Large fish, such as sharks, visit reefs often. They eat smaller fish that live there.

Other animals eat a reef's plants. Many plants, such as seaweeds and sea grasses, grow on reefs. The plants wave back and forth as water flows across a reef.

A whitetip reef shark hunts for food near a reef.

These light green plants are not really plants. They do not have roots or stems as plants do. But they grow all over reefs. They can even grow on rocks or animal shells. What are they?

Reefs are also full of algae (AL-jee). Algae are like plants with no roots or stems. Some algae look like tiny green hairs. Others are as large as seaweed. Algae get their energy from sunlight, as plants do. They grow in many places on a reef. The algae, plants, and animals that live on reefs are all important parts of Earth's oceans.

Some reefs are made of rock. How does this kind of reef form?

CHAPTER 2
WHAT MAKES A REEF?

Earth's surface is always changing. Sometimes the level of the ocean rises or falls. When the sea rises, water may cover a ridge of rocks on land. Then the rocks are under shallow water. If the rocks stay covered with water, they become a reef.

This sandy island is part of the Great Barrier Reef in Australia.

Moving water can create a reef. As the water flows, it picks up sand from the ocean floor. Later, it may drop the sand into piles. Several piles in a line form a ridge. The ridge may become high enough to reach the water's surface. Then it is called a reef.

Oyster shells make reefs too. Flowing ocean water carries baby oysters from one place to another. When the oysters land, they join their shells to rocks on the ocean floor. They grow and live in that spot. Often the baby oysters join their shells to the tops of other oysters. Over time, many oysters pile up. They form an oyster reef.

Oysters have two flat shells that open and close. Oysters can live in warm or cool water. So oyster reefs are found in both warm and cool parts of the ocean.

Turret coral polyps help build reefs. Most coral polyps are smaller than a pencil eraser.

A coral reef is made in a different way from other reefs. Coral polyps build coral reefs. Polyps are small sea animals that have soft, tube-shaped bodies. A polyp's mouth is at one end of its body. The mouth is surrounded by short tentacles (TEN-tuh-kuhlz). Tentacles are like thin, flexible arms.

Many kinds of coral polyps live in the ocean. Some corals are soft. They look like fans or trees. Other corals are hard. Only hard corals build reefs. That's because they have hard skeletons. A coral polyp's skeleton is on the outside of its body.

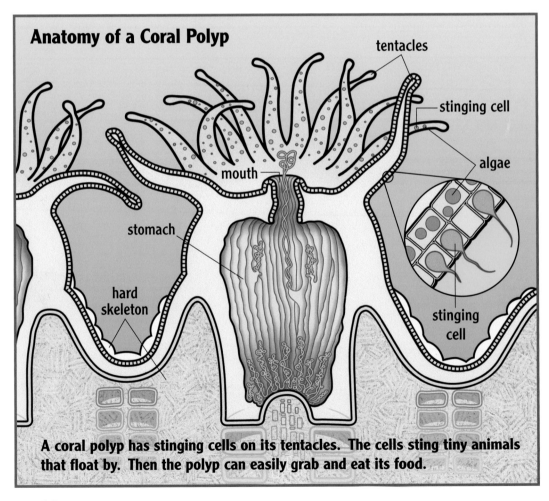

Anatomy of a Coral Polyp

tentacles

stinging cell

algae

mouth

stomach

hard skeleton

stinging cell

A coral polyp has stinging cells on its tentacles. The cells sting tiny animals that float by. Then the polyp can easily grab and eat its food.

This photo was taken through a microscope. The green circles are algae. If you lined up these algae next to one another, you would need about 2,500 to cover one inch!

Algae help coral polyps to make their skeletons. These algae live inside coral polyps. The algae are so tiny that you need a microscope to see them.

You can see the algae inside these coral polyps.

The algae inside the polyps take in
sunlight. The algae change the sunlight into
food for themselves. Then they give off
nutrients (NOO-tree-ents). Nutrients are
substances in food that keep plants and animals
healthy. The nutrients give polyps the energy
they need to build their hard skeletons.

To make food from light, algae use carbon dioxide (KAHR-buhn dye-OX-eyed) from the polyps. Carbon dioxide is a gas. Most animals make carbon dioxide when they breathe. A coral polyp also uses some of its own carbon dioxide to form its skeleton.

Coral gets its color from the algae that live inside it. The algae inside this hard elkhorn coral make it green.

The polyp makes its skeleton out of a hard substance called calcium carbonate (KAL-see-uhm KAHR-buh-nayt). To make this substance, a coral polyp takes calcium from the seawater.

Can you see why this hard coral is called brain coral?

Giant clams live on reefs. The shells of clams and oysters are made from the same hard substance that makes up coral skeletons.

The calcium combines with carbon dioxide inside the polyp's body. Together, they form calcium carbonate. Then the polyp can use this hard substance to build its skeleton.

Coral polyps attach their skeletons to other coral skeletons. They form a colony (KAH-luh-nee). A colony is a group of coral polyps that live close together, like people in an apartment building.

Many coral polyps live on a single branch of staghorn coral.

It can take thousands of years for coral colonies to form a reef.

New polyps keep building their skeletons on top of the colony. The skeletons of dead corals are left underneath. Over time, many colonies together form huge mounds and ridges. A ridge may reach near the water's surface. Then it has become a coral reef.

Coral polyps can't build a reef in this water. Polyps can live in only a certain kind of water. Where can coral reefs form?

CHAPTER 3

CORAL REEFS

Corals make many of Earth's most beautiful reefs. But coral reefs form only in certain places. The coral polyps that build reefs need warm salt water to survive. So coral reefs are found only in warm ocean water.

Coral polyps also need clean water. Ocean water flows through parts of a polyp's body. The water carries tiny, floating bits of food with it. The food gets caught in sticky parts of the polyp. The polyp eats these food bits. But mud and sand in the water can get caught in the polyp too. If they do, they can hurt the polyp. So corals can't form in muddy water.

Most polyps are unopened during the day, like the yellow cup coral polyps in the center of this photo. At night, they open up to catch food in their tentacles.

Hard corals depend on the algae inside them. Nutrients from the algae help the corals grow and build reefs.

Look at the brain coral on page 18. This is also brain coral. But these polyps are sticking out from their skeletons. They are catching food. Polyps get some of their nutrition from food and some from the algae inside them.

Most corals grow in shallow water. But mushroom soft coral can grow in water up to 4,000 feet deep.

The algae need sunlight to produce nutrients. So reef-building corals grow only in water where there is sunlight. Sunlight cannot reach deeper than about 330 feet underwater. Most hard corals live in water less than 250 feet deep.

Three main types of coral reefs exist. One type is called a fringing (FRIHN-jeeng) reef. It builds up along the coast of a large area of land. Shallow water separates the reef from the land. The side of a fringing reef that faces the ocean is very steep. The reef gets wider when coral is added to that side. Fringing reefs can grow to be a half mile wide.

From the air, you can see waves crashing along a fringing reef before they reach the land.

The Great Barrier Reef is more than 1,200 miles long.

A barrier (BARE-ee-uhr) reef is another kind of reef. It can be more than 10 miles away from land. Deep water separates a barrier reef from the land. The largest barrier reef in the world is the Great Barrier Reef. It is a chain of reefs near Australia.

An atoll (A-tahl) is a coral reef that is shaped like a ring. It forms after a reef has completely circled around a small island. Bit by bit, rain and waves wash away the island. After many years, water completely covers the island. But the reef still grows upward. Without the island in the middle, the reef looks like a ring. Then it is an atoll.

Atolls have formed where small islands used to be in the Indian Ocean.

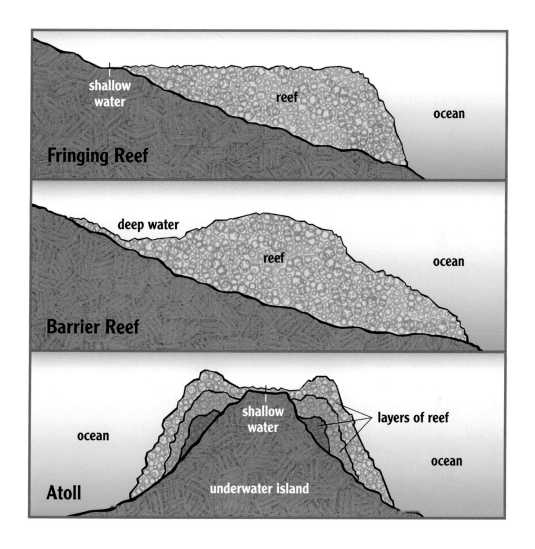

Fringing Reef — shallow water, reef, ocean

Barrier Reef — deep water, reef, ocean

Atoll — ocean, shallow water, layers of reef, ocean, underwater island

Sometimes a fourth type of reef forms. Small reefs may form in shallow water between a large reef and the land. They are called patch reefs. Patch reefs make circle shapes on the ocean floor.

These coral skeletons were discovered in the ground in Texas. Why would coral skeletons be in dry ground and not in water?

CHAPTER 4

FOSSIL REEFS

Look at a map of the United States. Find where Texas meets New Mexico. About 250 million years ago, water covered that area. A reef called Capitan Reef formed in the water over Texas. Capitan Reef was made of sponges. Sponges are a kind of sea animal. They have soft, rubbery bodies that are full of holes. Many kinds of shellfish from long ago also helped to build the reef. Some of them had two shells that fit together, like oysters' and clams' shells do. Others looked like bugs.

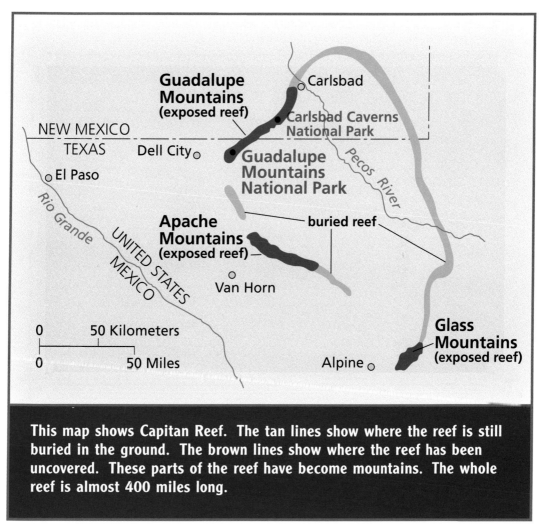

This map shows Capitan Reef. The tan lines show where the reef is still buried in the ground. The brown lines show where the reef has been uncovered. These parts of the reef have become mountains. The whole reef is almost 400 miles long.

After Capitan Reef formed, the water dried up. Then soil and rocks covered the reef. Over time, the shells and skeletons in the reef became fossils. Fossils are traces of plants or animals that have turned to stone. Capitan Reef became a fossil reef. Scientists found fossils of sea animals in this part of Texas. That's how they know that water used to be there.

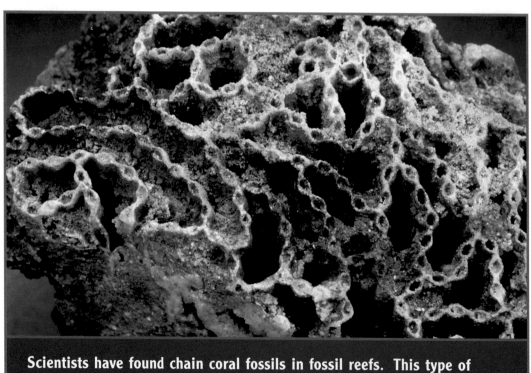

Scientists have found chain coral fossils in fossil reefs. This type of coral died out millions of years ago.

The Guadalupe Mountains in Texas were once underwater. They were part of Capitan Reef.

Scientists study fossil reefs to learn about Earth's history. They learn where water used to cover land. Fossil reefs also show how ocean life has changed over millions of years. Many of the creatures that lived on ancient reefs are extinct. Extinct means they have died out, like the dinosaurs. But scientists can learn about these animals by studying their fossils.

Strong winds and waves from hurricanes can harm people, animals, and buildings. How are big storms dangerous to ocean life?

CHAPTER 5

PEOPLE AND REEFS

Earth's reefs are in danger. Many are being hurt or broken. Scientists are concerned. Many fish and other creatures need the food and shelter of reefs in order to live.

Big storms such as hurricanes can harm a reef. Powerful waves crash into the reef and break off parts of it. Reefs can come back from this kind of damage. The plants and animals do return. But it takes a long time.

In 2004, a huge wave broke off this part of a fringing reef in the Indian Ocean. The wave was called a tsunami (soo-NAH-mee). It was caused by an earthquake.

This reef in Hawaii has become covered by algae.

Human waste is another danger to reefs. Some material from sewers goes into the ocean. The material often has a lot of nutrients in it. The nutrients help algae in the ocean water grow and spread. Too much algae can harm a coral reef. These algae block sunlight that the coral needs. Coral dies without enough sunlight.

Crown-of-thorns starfish can hurt coral reefs. These starfish eat coral polyps. Usually other fish eat the starfish. But in some places, fishers catch too many fish. Then there are fewer fish to eat the starfish. So more starfish grow. They feed on more corals. Crown-of-thorns starfish can kill large areas of a coral reef.

A crown-of-thorns starfish can destroy about 65 square feet of a coral reef in one year.

Dynamite blasts help fishers catch fish. They also hurt other life on reefs.

In other places, fishers blast dynamite in the water. The explosion stuns fish. Then they are easy to catch. But the explosions can also blast off large chunks of a reef.

Some fishers put poison into holes on a reef. They catch fish as they swim away from the poison. Dynamite and poison are harmful to coral and other animals that live on the reef.

A diver sprays a poison called cyanide (SY-uh-neyed) into a coral. Reef fish will swim out of the coral to escape the poison.

Coral reefs are also in danger because ocean water is getting warmer. Sunlight has always warmed the ocean. But scientists think more sunlight than ever is reaching the water. Certain chemicals in the air are making it easier for more sunlight to reach Earth. So the top layer of ocean water is getting warmer.

Air conditioners release chemicals that allow more sunlight to reach Earth. Some refrigerators do too.

Unusually warm ocean temperatures caused part of this coral to turn white.

Water that is too warm weakens the coral polyps. They can't make enough food to feed themselves and the algae inside them. So they force out the algae. Then the corals turn white. Scientists call this bleaching. Areas of a coral reef die if too many corals are bleached.

Even people who go diving for fun may harm reefs. Careless divers and their boats break off pieces of reefs by accident. And coral polyps can die if people stand on them.

Some reefs have become protected by laws. The laws may keep people from removing coral, polluting, boating, fishing, or diving near a protected reef. Without those dangers, the reef will stay healthier. Scientists can study it more.

Shells and pieces of coral are often collected to sell to tourists. Breaking off coral pieces is harmful to a reef.

Many people enjoy going diving near reefs. But they must be careful not to harm a reef's plants or animals.

Earth's oceans have more than 10,000 reefs. Reefs are places of beauty. They are full of ocean life. And they are important parts of Earth's oceans. People must work together to help reefs remain healthy.

ON SHARING A BOOK

When you share a book with a child, you show that reading is important. To get the most out of the experience, read in a comfortable, quiet place. Turn off the television and limit other distractions, such as telephone calls. Be prepared to start slowly. Take turns reading parts of this book. Stop occasionally and discuss what you're reading. Talk about the photographs. If the child begins to lose interest, stop reading. When you pick up the book again, revisit the parts you have already read.

BE A VOCABULARY DETECTIVE

The word list on page 5 contains words that are important in understanding the topic of this book. Be word detectives and search for the words as you read the book together. Talk about what the words mean and how they are used in the sentence. Do any of these words have more than one meaning? You will find the words defined in a glossary on page 46.

WHAT ABOUT QUESTIONS?

Use questions to make sure the child understands the information in this book. Here are some suggestions:

> What did this paragraph tell us? What does this picture show? What do you think we'll learn about next? How does an oyster reef form? Where do coral polyps build reefs? Can you name one type of coral reef? What are some of the dangers to reefs? What is your favorite part of the book? Why?

If the child has questions, don't hesitate to respond with questions of your own, such as What do *you* think? Why? What is it that you don't know? If the child can't remember certain facts, turn to the index.

INTRODUCING THE INDEX

The index helps readers find information without searching through the whole book. Turn to the index on page 48. Choose an entry such as *algae* and ask the child to use the index to find out how algae inside coral polyps help to keep the polyps healthy. Repeat with as many entries as you like. Ask the child to point out the differences between an index and a glossary. (The index helps readers find information, while the glossary tells readers what words mean.)

LEARN MORE ABOUT
REEFS

BOOKS
Cole, Joanna. *The Magic School Bus Takes a Dive: A Book about Coral Reefs.* **New York: Scholastic, 1998.**

Gray, Susan H. *Coral Reefs.* **Minneapolis: Compass Point Books, 2001.**

Rhodes, Mary Jo, and David Hall. *Life on a Coral Reef.* **New York: Children's Press, 2006.**

Walker, Sally M. *Fossils.* **Minneapolis: Lerner Publications Company, 2007.**

WEBSITES
NOAA Photo Library—Coral Kingdom
http://www.photolib.noaa.gov/reef/
Visit this website to see colorful photos of the animals that live in coral reefs around the world.

Reef Relief—Children's Resources
http://www.reefrelief.org/kids/index.shtml
Print out pictures of several reef fish, color them, and read the descriptions of each fish to learn more. You can also print out and color a picture of a whole coral reef.

***Time* for Kids: The Coral Reef Crisis**
http://www.timeforkids.com/TFK/magazines/story/0,6277,59711,00.html
This article explains why coral reefs are in danger and why they must be saved.

GLOSSARY

algae (AL-jee): plant-like growths with no roots or stems. They grow underwater and in other damp places.

atoll (A-tahl): a ring-shaped coral reef

barrier (BARE-ee-uhr) reef: a coral reef separated from land by a wide, deep area of water

calcium carbonate (KAL-see-uhm KAHR-buh-nayt): the hard substance that makes up a coral polyp's frame. This skeleton is made from calcium and carbon dioxide.

carbon dioxide (KAHR-buhn dye-OX-eyed): a gas that is produced when animals breathe

colony (KAH-luh-nee): a group of coral polyps that live close together

coral polyps (KOR-uhl PAH-lihps): tiny sea animals that build coral reefs by joining their hard skeletons to one another

extinct: no longer existing. If a type of plant or animal completely dies out, it becomes extinct.

fossils: shells, skeletons, or other traces of animals and plants that lived long ago. In fossils, these traces have turned to stone over a long period of time.

fringing (FRIHN-jeeng) reef: a coral reef that forms along a coastline. It is separated from the land by shallow water.

tentacles (TEN-tuh-kuhlz): thin, flexible arms. A coral polyp uses its tentacles to grab food.

INDEX

Pages listed in **bold** type refer to photographs.